My First Pocket Guide

Indiana

By Carole Marsh

Correlates with Indiana's Academic Standards

The Indiana Experience

The GALLOPADE GANG

Carole Marsh
Bob Longmeyer
Chad Beard
Cecil Anderson
Steven Saint-Laurent
Karin Petersen
Billie Walburn
Doug Boston
Jill Sanders
William Nesbitt, Jr.
Kathy Zimmer
Wanda Coats
Terry Briggs
Pam Dufresne
Cranston Davenport
Lisa Stanley
Antoinette Miller
Victoria DeJoy
Jackie Clayton

Published by
GALLOPADE
INTERNATIONAL

www.indianaexperience.com
800-536-2GET • www.gallopade.com

Gallopade is proud to be a member of these educational organizations and associations:

NSSEA

SHOPA MEMBER™
School, Home, & Office Products Association

Other Indiana Experience Products

- The Indiana Experience!
- The BIG Indiana Reproducible Activity Book
- The Indiana Coloring Book
- My First Book About Indiana!
- Indiana "Jography": A Fun Run Through Our State
- Indiana Jeopardy!: Answers and Questions About Our State
- The Indiana Experience! Sticker Pack
- The Indiana Experience! Poster/Map
- Discover Indiana CD-ROM
- Indiana "Geo" Bingo Game
- Indiana "Histo" Bingo Game

A Word From the Author... (okay, a few words)...

Hi!

Here's your own handy pocket guide about the great state of Indiana! It really will fit in a pocket–I tested it. And it really will be useful when you want to know a fact you forgot, to bone up for a test, or when your teacher says, "I wonder . . ." and you have the answer–instantly! Wow, I'm impressed!

Get smart, have fun!

Carole Marsh

Indiana Basics explores your state's symbols and their special meanings!

Indiana Geography digs up the what's where in your state!

Indiana History is like traveling through time to some of your state's great moments!

Indiana People introduces you to famous personalities and your next-door neighbors!

Indiana Places shows you where you might enjoy your next family vacation!

Indiana Nature - no preservatives here, just what Mother Nature gave to prototype!

All the real fun stuff that we just HAD to save for its own section!

Who Named You?

Indiana's official state name is . . .

State Name

Indiana

OFFICIAL: appointed, authorized, or approved by a government or organization

Statehood: December 11, 1816

Indiana was the 19th state to ratify the Constitution.

Land of the Indians

Indiana means "Land of the Indians." Many of these Native Americans inhabited the forests of early Indiana. Presently, there are less than 8,000 Native Americans living in the state.

What's In A Name?

Indiana is known by a few nicknames. The most popular one is

The Hoosier State

Other nicknames include:

Crossroads of America
Main Street of the Midwest
Heartland of America

Origin of Nickname

There are several legends as to the origin of the nickname "Hoosier." One legend says that when Indiana pioneers had a visitor knock on their cabin door, the settlers would answer, **"Who's yere?"** which later turned into "Hoosier." Another legend states that Indiana rivermen were so successful at beating, or "hushing," their enemies in a fight that they became known as **"hushers."** Still another tale is told that Samuel Hoosier, the boss for a canal-building crew, only hired men from Indiana. These men were called **"Hoosier's men."**

John Finley of Richmond popularized the term "Hoosier" in his poem "The Hoosier's Nest," which appeared in Indianapolis newspapers in 1813. Whatever its origin, the nickname is widely used today to refer to natives of Indiana!

State Capital: Indianapolis

State Capital/ Capitol

While Indiana was still a territory, Vincennes was the capital. The first state capital was in southern Indiana, in the town of Corydon. In 1820, developers chose an undeveloped site near the center of the state to serve as a new capital city. The new capital city was named Indianapolis and was designed with four major diagonal streets leading to a city center of government buildings. Indianapolis became the official state capital in 1825.

When deciding on a name for the new state capital, many legislators wanted to call it "Tecumseh" after the famous Indian chief!

Word Definition

CAPITAL: a town or city that is the official seat of government
CAPITOL: the building in which the government officials meet

Who's in Charge Here?

Indiana's GOVERNMENT has three branches:

LEGISLATIVE	EXECUTIVE	JUDICIAL
The legislative branch is called the General Assembly. Two Houses: The Senate (50 members elected to 4-year terms) House of Representatives (100 members elected to 2-year terms)	A governor, lieutenant governor, secretary of state, treasurer, attorney general, auditor, and department heads	A chief justice plus four associate justices Court of Appeals, Circuit Courts, Superior Courts, Probate Courts, Criminal Courts

All but one of Indiana's 92 counties are governed by a three-member board of county commissioners. Counties include cities, towns and townships. Cities are governed by a mayor and a council. Towns are governed by a board of trustees. In townships, a township trustee is elected to serve along with an advisory board.

State Flag

Indiana's flag was adopted in 1917.

The state flag features a golden torch and flame with golden stars against a field of blue. The torch stands for liberty and enlightenment, and the rays for their far-reaching effects. The outer circle of 13 stars symbolizes the original states. The five stars of the inner circle stand for the next five states to enter the Union. The star directly above the torch represents Indiana as the 19th state to enter the Union. The word "Indiana" is in a half-circle above the state star.

State Seal and Motto

State Seal

Indiana's state seal was adopted in 1963

The Indiana state motto, "Crossroads of America," can be traced back to the early 1800s. The Ohio River and various canals provided water transportation, and the National Road provided ground transportation. Railroads also began to criss-cross the state. Today, Indiana has more miles of interstate highway per square mile than any other state. Also, more major highways intersect in Indiana than in any other state. Indiana is most definitely the "Crossroads of America!"

State Motto

Indiana's state motto is...

Crossroads of America

Word Definition

MOTTO: a sentence, phrase, or word expressing the spirit or purpose of an organization or group

Birds of Red Feathers

The state bird of Indiana is the cardinal, *Cardinalis cardinalis,* known for its bright plumage and cheerful song.

Cardinals live in Indiana year-round. The male is a bright red, and the female is brown with a dull red crest, wings, and tail. The Cardinal was named the state bird in 1933.

Tulip Tree

"I think that I shall never see a poem as lovely as a tree."
—Joyce Kilmer

The Tulip Tree, also known as the yellow poplar, is actually a member of the magnolia family! Tulip Trees can be found throughout Indiana. Their roundish leaves and bell-shaped flowers bloom in early May or June. These trees grow tall and straight and have soft, white wood. The Tulip Tree became the state tree in 1931.

State Flower

Peony

Indiana's state flower blooms in late May or early June. Peonies tend to be bushy plants that have large, beautiful blossoms in various shades of red, pink, and white.

The Peony is actually Indiana's fourth state flower! The first three were the carnation, the tulip tree blossom, and the zinnia. In 1957, the general assembly chose the Peony to be the state flower.

State Poem

"Indiana"

God crowned her hills with beauty,
Gave her lakes and winding streams,
Then He edged them all with woodlands
As the settings for our dreams.
Lovely are her moonlit rivers,
Shadowed by the sycamores,
Where the fragrant winds of Summer
Play along the willowed shores.
I must roam those wooded hillsides,
I must heed the native call,
For a Pagan voice within me
Seems to answer to it all.
I must walk where squirrels scamper
Down a rustic old rail fence,
Where a choir of birds is singing
In the woodland. . . green and dense.
I must learn more of my homeland
For it's paradise to me,
There's no haven quite as peaceful,
There's no place I'd rather be.
Indiana . . . is a garden
Where the seeds of peace have grown,
Where each tree, and vine, and flower
Has a beauty . . . all its own.
Lovely are the fields and meadows,
That reach out to hills that rise
Where the dreamy Wabash River
Wanders on . . . through paradise.

by Arthur Franklin Mapes, adopted in 1963

Limestone

The Indiana state rock is Limestone. Found in central and southern Indiana, Limestone is mined from quarries and used in the construction of buildings throughout the state and nation. The Indiana state capitol building was made from Indiana Limestone. Many famous buildings outside of Indiana have also been made from Indiana Limestone: the Empire State Building and Rockefeller Center in New York City, as well as the Washington National Cathedral, Pentagon, and United States Treasury in Washington, D.C. This sturdy and beautiful material has been used to make several other government buildings in Washington, D.C. and various states.

Riddle: What do you get when you cross the state rock with a popular dessert?

Answer: A Key Limestone Pie!

Hoosier Hysteria!

Indiana is known far and wide as the "Home of Basketball." From the young to the old, basketball "scores" big points as a Hoosier pastime. Assembly Hall at Indiana University in Bloomington is the center of Indiana basketball. Fans dressed in red and white cheer the Hoosiers on.

High school basketball can be just as intense as any IU game when tournament time rolls around. Although Indiana is loaded with powerhouse teams, everyone remembers the 1954 state championship between mighty Muncie Central High and tiny Milan High. This classic story was immortalized in the 1987 film, *Hoosiers*. Often called the "Milan Miracle," this underdog team became a high school legend when Bobby Plump sank a —GASP!—last-second shot to win the championship.

State Song

"On the Banks of the Wabash, Far Away"

words and music by Paul Dresser

State Song

'ROUND MY INDIANA HOMESTEAD
WAVE THE CORNFIELDS,
IN THE DISTANCE LOOM THE WOODLANDS
CLEAR AND COOL.
OFTENTIMES MY THOUGHTS REVERT
TO SCENES OF CHILDHOOD,
WHERE I FIRST RECEIVED MY
LESSONS, NATURE'S SCHOOL.

OH, THE MOONLIGHT'S FAIR TONIGHT
ALONG THE WABASH,
FROM THE FIELDS THERE COMES THE
BREATH OF NEW-MOWN HAY,
THROUGH THE SYCAMORES THE CANDLE
LIGHTS ARE GLEAMING,
ON THE BANKS OF THE WABASH, FAR AWAY . . .

A Bounty of Bridges

Parke County is called the Covered Bridge Capital of the World. Originally, it had more than 50 covered bridges, but many were lost to natural deterioration, floods, and fires. Today, Parke County has 32 intact, authentic covered bridges. The two oldest bridges date back to 1856 while the newest bridge was built in 1920. All 32 bridges were placed on the National Register of Historic Sites in 1978. Most of the covered bridges still support traffic. Beginning in 1957, the county has hosted a ten-day Covered Bridge Festival. This nationally recognized event regularly entices some 500,000 visitors!

Riddle: What happens when the Wabash River floods?

Answer: It gets too big for its bridges!

Wabash River

The Wabash River rises in Ohio and flows west and south across the entire state of Indiana. It is part of the Indiana-Illinois border, where it flows into the Ohio River. It is 512 miles (824 kilometers) in length. With its tributaries, the Wabash drains more than two-thirds of Indiana's rain and snow. Paralleling the river, the Wabash and Erie Canal opened in 1837 and was the longest canal ever built in the country. The popular term "Wabash Cannon Ball" came from a 1940s song about a train on the Wabash Railroad, which was situated alongside the river. The Wabash River is near and dear to Hoosiers' hearts not only because of the important role it played in Indiana's settlement, but because its beauty is memorialized in the state song.

State Map

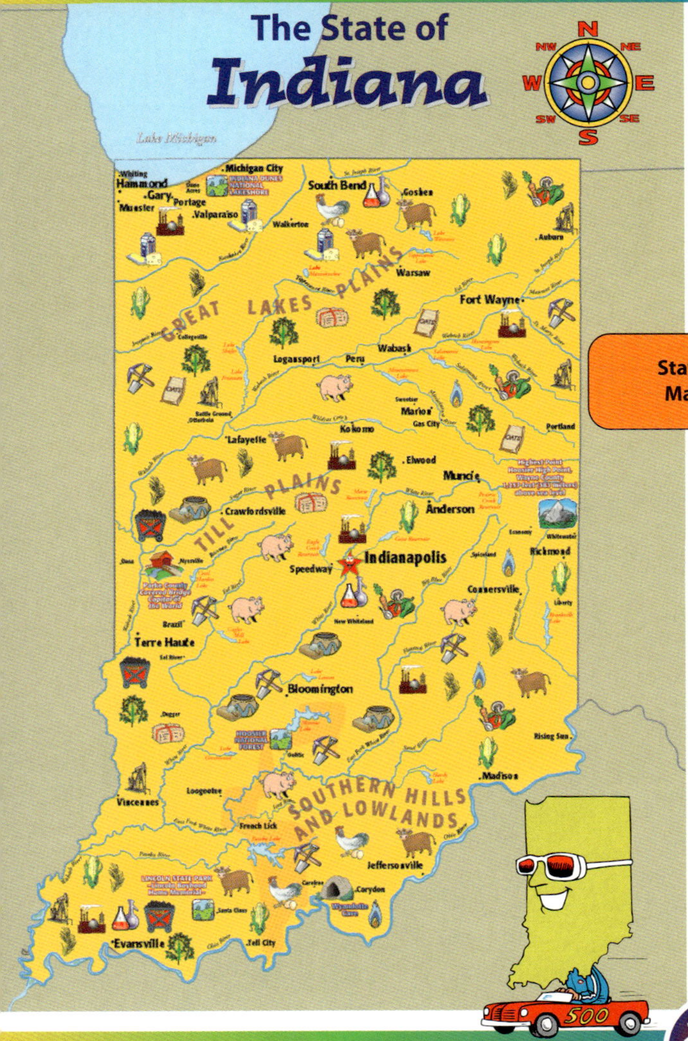

State Map

State Location

Indiana is a Midwestern state, located in America's heartland.

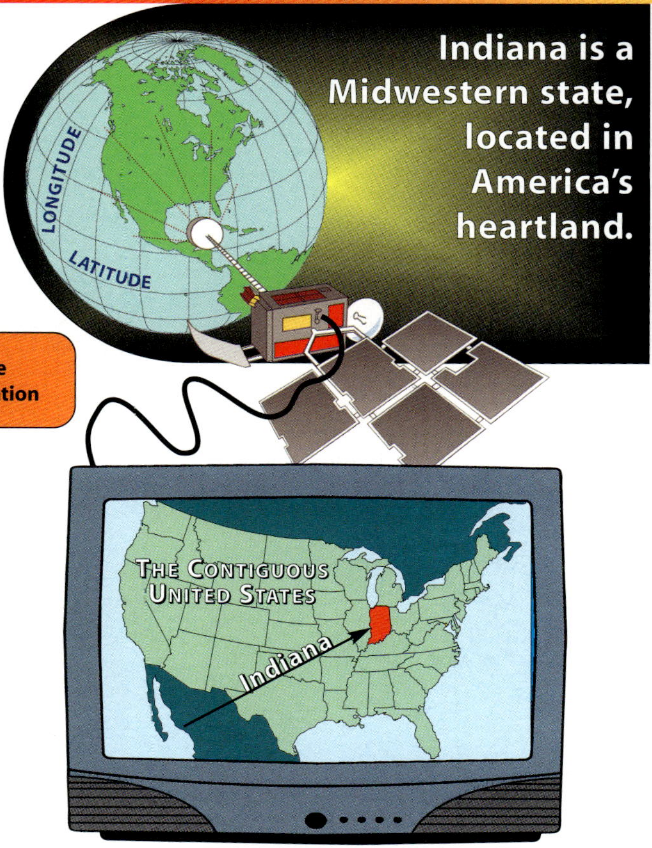

Word Definition

LATITUDE: Imaginary lines which run horizontally east and west around the globe
LONGITUDE: Imaginary lines which run vertically north and south around the globe

On The Border!

These border Indiana:

States: Ohio, Illinois, Kentucky, Michigan

Bodies of water: Lake Michigan, Ohio River, Wabash River

I'll Take the Low Road...

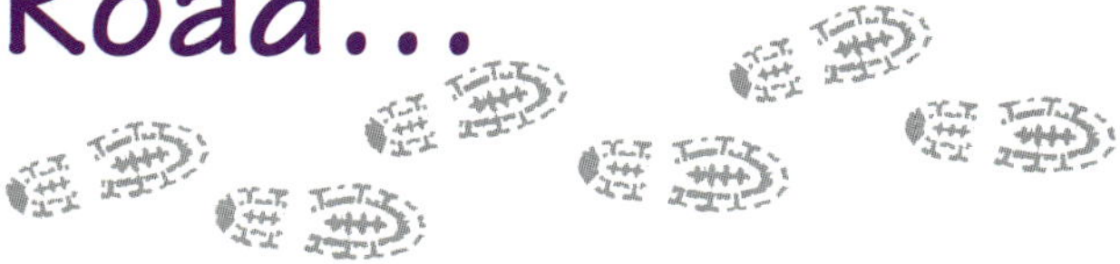

Indiana is 285 miles (459 kilometers) north to south... or south to north. Either way, it's a long drive!

Total Area: Approx. 36,420 square miles (94,320 square kilometers)
Land Area: Approx. 35,870 square miles (92,896 square kilometers)

Indiana is 177 miles (285 kilometers) east to west ... or west to east. That's shorter than driving the length of the state, but it will still take awhile!

You Take the High Road!

HIGHEST POINT

Hoosier High Point, Wayne County–1,257 feet (383 meters) above sea level

The Hoosier High Point was named in 1993 by the General Assembly of the State of Indiana. The highpoint is on private property.

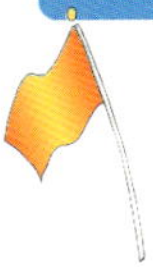

LOWEST POINT

Posey County–320 feet (98 meters) above sea level

I'm County-ing on You!

Indiana is divided into 92 counties.

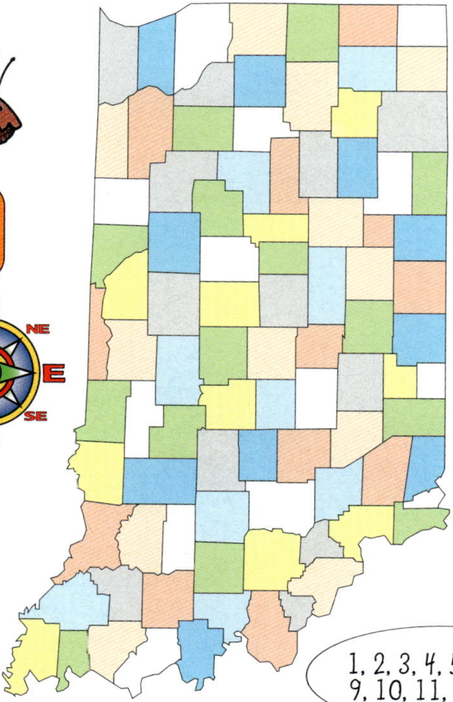

Word Definition

COUNTY: an administrative subdivision of a state or territory

Natural Resources

NATURAL RESOURCES:
things that exist in or are formed by nature

Word Definition

More than 100 species of trees live in Indiana. Before the settlers arrived, 80 percent of the state was covered with forests. Today, only about 17 percent of Indiana is considered forested. Much of this land is contained in state forests and the Hoosier National Forest. Most forested areas are located in the southern part of the state.

Bituminous coal is the main mineral produced in Indiana. Indiana is the eighth leading coal-producing state in the nation. Most of the state's coal comes from western and southwestern Indiana.

Limestone is also an important natural resource in Indiana!

Weather, Or Not?!

Indiana is blessed to have four distinct and beautiful seasons. Most of the state has a humid climate. This provides long, warm summers in which to enjoy the many "swimming holes" throughout the state. The fall ushers in a terrific rainbow of colors with oak, maple, yellow poplar, and many other trees showing off their amazing leaves. During the winter months, an average of 20 inches (51 centimeters) of snow falls throughout the state. Northern Indiana, near Lake Michigan, receives a lot of "lake effect" snow, but the lake keeps temperatures milder than would be expected. Spring is tornado season throughout the Midwest, with Indiana having its fair share. Sometimes, spring rains can make the Ohio River swell and flooding can be a concern in many river towns.

Highest temperature: 116°F (47°C), Collegeville

°F=Degrees Fahrenheit °C=Degrees Celsius

Lowest temperature: -36°F (-38°C), New Whiteland

Topography

BACK ON TOP

Indiana's topography includes these major regions:

NORTH: Great Lakes Plains—characterized by several areas of flat or marshy land, as well as areas that are high and hilly; moraines (high ridges) and sand dunes located near Lake Michigan

CENTRAL: Till Plains—made up of fertile, rolling plains with deposits of sand, gravel and limestone

SOUTH: Southern Hills and Lowlands—home of forested hills and valleys that include bedrock and limestone

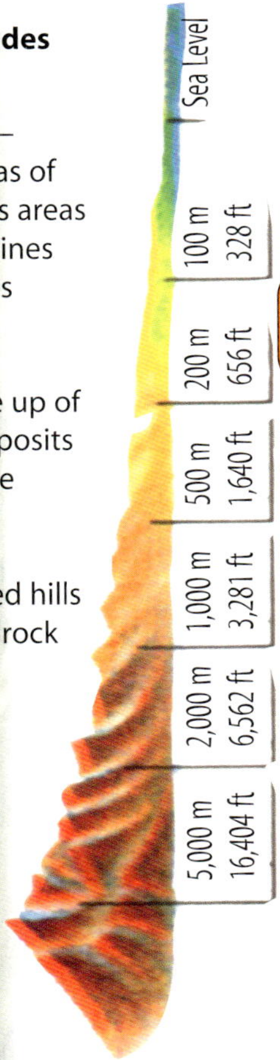

Word Definition

TOPOGRAPHY: the detailed mapping of the features of a small area or district

Mounds Abound in Indiana!

At least one-third of all counties in Indiana contain remains of ancient mounds, evidence of an early Indian culture. These earthen mounds were built for religious purposes and also for burial sites. The most famous mound site in the state is *Angel Mounds*, near Evansville. People of the Mississippian culture built these mounds near their thriving village. They inhabited the area from 1100 to 1450. Angel Mounds is named after Mathias Angel and his descendants, who once owned the land.

Another popular mound site, near Anderson, is located atop limestone bluffs overlooking the White River. Eleven prehistoric earthworks are preserved at *Mounds State Park*. The most awesome is the circular *Great Mound*. It is nearly 1,200 feet (366 meters) around and 9 feet (2.7 meters) high. The shapes of some of the other mounds are interesting—one is shaped like a cone, two are shaped like a guitar, and yet another is U-shaped! The Adena and Hopewell Indians are believed to have built these ancient mounds.

Down the River

Most of Indiana's rivers flow southward and westward to form part of the Mississippi River system. There are also several small rivers that flow northward toward Lake Michigan or eastward, through Ohio, to Lake Erie.

The Ohio River forms the entire southern border of Indiana, separating it from the state of Kentucky.

Indiana's Lost River travels 22 miles (35 kilometers) underground!

Here are some of Indiana's major rivers:

- **Ohio**
- **Wabash**
- **White**
- **Tippecanoe**
- **Kankakee**
- **Maumee**
- **St. Joseph**
- **St. Marys**
- **Salamonie**
- **Mississinewa**
- **Eel**

Gone Fishin'

- Lake Wawasee
- Monroe Lake
- Geist Reservoir
- Eagle Creek Reservoir
- Patoka Lake
- Brookville Lake
- Manitau Lake
- Turkey Lake
- Maxinkuckee Lake
- Huntington Reservoir

Word Definition

RESERVOIR: a body of water stored for public use

ARE YOU A CITY MOUSE... OR COUNTRY MOUSE?

Have you heard these wonderful Indiana city, town, and crossroad names? Perhaps you can start your own list!

LARGER TOWNS:

Indianapolis
Fort Wayne
Evansville
South Bend
Gary
Terre Haute
Hammond
Anderson
Elkhart
Lafayette

SMALLER TOWNS:

French Lick
Economy
Twelve Mile
Doolittle Mills
Young America
Hope
Santa Claus
Patriot
Paoli
Speed
Farmland
Needmore

Transportation

Major Interstate Highways

I-70, I-74, I-69, I-65,
I-64, I-80/90
Indiana has more miles of interstate highways than any other state!

Railroads

Northern Indiana is criss-crossed by all the major rail lines to Chicago from the eastern United States. This area has one of the greatest concentrations of railroad tracks in the country.

Transportation

Major Airports

Almost every major city in Indiana is served by a commercial airport. Indianapolis has the busiest airport in the state. It serves more than 2.7 million passengers each year.

Seaports

The Port of Indiana, a deepwater port at Burns Harbor on Lake Michigan, opened in 1970. It was a boost to the state's economy because it provided a port along the St. Lawrence Seaway to service oceangoing vessels from the Atlantic Ocean.

Timeline

- 600 BC Ancient Mississippian Indian tribe settles along Ohio River
- 1679 René-Robert Cavelier, Sieur de La Salle, sails into St. Joseph River
- 1700 Various Indian tribes from the East settle in Indiana
- 1732 Jesuit missionaries found Vincennes, first permanent Indiana settlement
- 1754 French and Indian War begins
- 1779 George Rogers Clark wins Fort Sackville and Vincennes from British during American Revolution
- 1787 Indiana becomes part of Northwest Territory
- 1811 William Henry Harrison defeats the Shawnee Prophet at the Battle of Tippecanoe
- 1816 Indiana becomes the 19th state on December 11
- 1825 Indianapolis becomes the state's new capital
- 1861 Civil War begins
- 1906 U.S. Steel lays out plans to build Gary
- 1911 First Indianapolis 500 race held
- 1930s Farms fail after WWI and 1929 stock market crash
- 1956 Indiana Toll Road joins eastern and western borders of the state
- 1970 Port of Indiana opens on Lake Michigan
- 1987 Pan American Games held in Indianapolis
- 1989 Indiana native Dan Quayle becomes vice-president under George Bush
- 2001 Indiana enters the 21st century!

Here come the humans!

Early History

More than 10,000 years ago, wandering bands of hunters came to the area that would one day become the state of Indiana. They were in search of wild game. This culture, known as the Archaic, were the ancestors of Indiana's Native American population.

The first inhabitants of the Great Lakes region may have hunted the now-extinct mammoth and mastodon. These animals resembled elephants but were very hairy and had large tusks.

Native Americans Once Ruled!

The Indian tribes of the state of Indiana included the *Miami*, *Potawatomi*, *Delaware*, *Kickapoo*, and *Shawnee*. Many of these early tribes arrived from the eastern states because they were being pushed off their land there. Most tribes only stayed in the Indiana territory for 25 to 50 years before moving further west. The *Miami* Indian tribe established the most permanent roots in Indiana, living in the state for almost 150 years. *Little Turtle* was a respected Miami chief and superb military leader. Other well-known Indian chiefs of Indiana were *Pontiac*, of the Ottawas, *Tecumseh*, of the Shawnee, and the *Shawnee Prophet*, Tecumseh's brother.

Word Definition

WAMPUM: beads, pierced and strung, used by Indians as money, or for ornaments or ceremonies.

Land Ho!

The French were the first to explore Indiana. René-Robert Cavelier, Sieur de La Salle, was the first known European to set foot in the state. In 1679, he claimed lands for France and searched for a waterway that would take him all the way to the Pacific Ocean.

The next Frenchmen to arrive were fur traders, often called *voyageurs*. They set up trading posts in the 1720s, where they traded items with the Indians in return for furs. Following the fur traders were the Jesuit Catholic missionaries. They founded the settlement of Vincennes around 1732.

When English settlers arrived in present-day Indiana, conflicts with the French and the Indians resulted. In 1754, the French and Indian War began, pitting the French and Indians against the British. In 1763, the war ended, with the British the victors. France gave Britain most of its land east of the Mississippi River, including what is now Indiana.

Struggle for Statehood

Although the French had been friendly with the Indians, the British had no such intention. The Indians had regarded the French as brothers, but now viewed the British as rulers. Many forts were attacked by Indians soon after the British took command. After the American Revolution, an increase in settlers angered many Indian tribes, which resulted in more attacks, especially by the bold Miami chief Little Turtle.

Frustrated by constant setbacks, President George Washington sent the famous Revolutionary War general "Mad Anthony Wayne" to take charge. In 1794, Little Turtle was defeated at the Battle of Fallen Timbers in Ohio. General Anthony Wayne returned to Indiana and built Fort Wayne over the site of a Miami village.

Early Settlement

In 1811, while the great Shawnee chief Tecumseh was away from camp, General William Henry Harrison marched his troops toward the Indian camp. Tecumseh's brother, the Shawnee Prophet, rallied the Indians to battle and the famous Battle of Tippecanoe followed. General Harrison's troops were victorious. This battle, and others that followed, put an end to Indian resistance throughout the Northwest Territory.

William Henry Harrison

By 1815, more than 60,000 pioneers lived in the Indiana territory. Once its boundaries were fixed by Congress, Indiana was eligible to become a state. On December 11, 1816, Indiana became the 19th state admitted to the Union.

CORN & SOYBEANS

Corn has historically been a leading crop in Indiana's farming industry and this remains true today. Indiana is part of the Midwestern Corn Belt. Most years, almost half of all cropland is planted in corn. In recent years, another crop has rapidly increased in amount and value—soybeans. Any Hoosier knows that a drive through the country in late summer will show fields of stocky, green soybeans or tall, tasseled cornstalks.

Many kinds of corn are grown throughout the state such as feed corn (for animals), sweet corn (for humans), and popcorn. In 1997, Indiana was the number one producer of popcorn in the nation!

Ask an adult to help make the following recipe.

POPCORN BALLS:

6 quarts air-popped popcorn
1 cup light Karo syrup
1 teaspoon vinegar
2 tablespoons butter
3 1/2 cups brown sugar
1/2 teaspoon baking soda (dissolved in tablespoon of hot water)

Directions:

Heat Karo syrup, vinegar, brown sugar, and butter together until thickened. Add dissolved baking soda to mixture. Pour mixture over popcorn and stir. Form into balls. Enjoy!

Fact Or Fiction?

- During the spring of 1949, tales of a giant turtle spread throughout the town of Churubusco, Indiana. A local farmer reported seeing a turtle as large as a dining room table in a lake on his land! A massive hunt for the turtle followed, but none was ever found. The "Beast of 'Busco" is still remembered in the community by a Turtle Days festival each June.

- It was Christmas Eve 1889 on a farm near South Bend. Eleven-year-old Oliver Larch was sent outside to fetch water from the family well. A few minutes later, Oliver's screams could be heard and his family rushed outside to investigate. They clearly heard young Oliver's voice high above their heads shouting, "Help! They've got me!" They frantically searched, but could find him nowhere. The boy's footprints in the snow simply ended and the bucket that he had carried with him lay beside his trail. Oliver Larch was never seen again!

Legends & Lore

- The beautiful and exotic raintree is believed to grow somewhere in Henry County. This tree supposedly holds the secret of life and was planted by Johnny Appleseed on his travels throughout the Midwest. Perhaps you can find the raintree and "stand beneath its rain of golden blossoms."

Revolution

Freedom!

On the East Coast, things were getting tense between the British and American colonists. Tired of strict rule and unfair taxes, the colonists went to war with Britain to gain their independence. When the *American Revolution* broke out in 1775, settlers in Indiana joined in the fight for freedom.

A Virginia officer named *George Rogers Clark* marched into Indiana with his troops in 1778, winning Fort Sackville from the British. The British, led by *Henry Hamilton*, recaptured the fort. Clark retreated to rally his men for another try. In 1779, during the harsh Hoosier winter, Clark and his men defeated the British and took Fort Sackville again. This victory caused present-day Indiana to become American soil and guaranteed George Rogers Clark hero status in Indiana. The *Treaty of Paris* in 1783 formally ended the American Revolution.

Revolution

Henry Hamilton, British governor of the territory including Indiana, was often called "Hair Buyer Hamilton." His hatred for the Americans led him to encourage Indians to take American scalps.

Of Human Bondage

As the Civil War approached, many people in southern Indiana defended the rights of southerners to own slaves. However, residents of northern Indiana, as well as the state's many Quaker groups, were very much against slavery. Wayne County, Indiana was the home of the *"Grand Central Station of the Underground Railroad."* Members of this Underground Railroad were people throughout the community, as well as other parts of Indiana and other states, who secretly helped slaves escape to freedom. Levi and Katie Coffin were two famous conductors of the Underground Railroad. The Coffins were Quakers living in Fountain City who estimated that they provided overnight lodging for more than 2,000 runaway slaves in the years before the Civil War.

Pro-southern Hoosiers saw the Coffins as lawbreakers. The state constitution of 1850, written mainly by these sympathizers, made it illegal to assist an escaped slave. A clause was added in 1851 that forbade blacks from settling in Indiana.

One of the 2,000 or more slaves who rested at the Coffin House was Eliza, the heroine of Harriet Beecher Stowe's *Uncle Tom's Cabin*

Word Definition

ABOLITIONIST: person who believed slavery was wrong and should be abolished.

The Civil War

Brother

The Civil War was fought over slavery and the right of the states to make their own individual decisions. Southern states, with plantations and slaves, were on one side of the battle. Northern states, who opposed slavery or had no need for it, were on the other side. Some states remained neutral on the issue.

Although many Hoosiers were divided on the issue of slavery, the great majority rallied around the former Hoosier, President Abraham Lincoln, as he sought volunteers for the Union army. An amazing number of Hoosiers answered the call and joined the Union army. As the Civil War raged, the total number of Hoosier soldiers soared to 200,000. These loyal men were determined to keep America together. Only New York contributed more soldiers to the Union cause. Thousands of Hoosier soldiers were wounded in battle and more than 25,000 were killed. The bloody Civil War cost Indiana more lives than any other conflict.

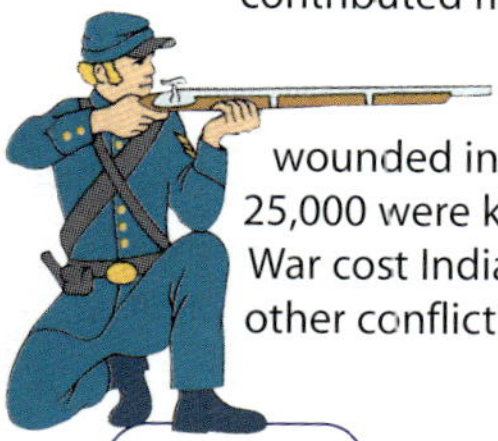

Word Definition

RECONSTRUCTION: the recovery and rebuilding period following the Civil War.

vs. Brother

The Civil War was also called the War Between the States. Soldiers often found themselves fighting against former friends and neighbors, even brother against brother. Those who did survive often went home without an arm, leg, or both, since amputation was the "cure" for most battlefield wounds. More Americans were killed during the Civil War than during World Wars I and II combined!

The only time the war reached Indiana was when Confederate General John Hunt Morgan led his cavalrymen, called Morgan's Raiders, to Corydon and throughout the Indiana countryside, robbing farmhouses and looting stores.

Get It In Writing!

Northwest Ordinance, 1787
established the Northwest Territory

First State Constitution, 1816

Amended State Constitution, 1851
provision barring blacks from
entering the state is added

Amended State Constitution, 1881
provision barring blacks from
entering the state is repealed

WELCOME TO AMERICA!

Most of Indiana's early immigrants came from England, Scotland and Wales. The second wave of immigrants came from the South and made their homes in southern Indiana. After this southern wave of immigration, came a northern wave from New York, Pennsylvania, and other eastern states.

A safe haven for religious groups, Indiana attracted the Quakers, or Society of Friends. They arrived in 1807 and established a community in Richmond. Amish and Mennonite people from Germany and Switzerland also found a safe religious haven in Indiana in the early 1800s. Most of them settled in the northeastern counties, where they still thrive today.

Many immigrants during the middle 1800s arrived from Germany and Ireland. Steel mills and other heavy industries attracted people from countries like Poland, Hungary, Belgium, and Italy. African-Americans were also drawn to the northern industrial cities.

Only a small percentage of Indiana's residents today are immigrants. Most of these recent immigrants come from Mexico, Canada, Germany, Great Britain, and Southeast Asia. Many of these immigrants eventually become U.S. citizens.

Swoosh!

1917

Long Path Tornado races through Illinois and Indiana; holds the record for the longest time of a single twister–7 hours!

1925

Tri-State Tornado hits Indiana, Illinois and Missouri; one of the deadliest single tornados in U.S. history; kills 74 people in Indiana alone

1937

Ohio River flood covers two-thirds of Evansville with water; 90,000 people forced from their homes

1968

Downtown Richmond gas explosion kills 41 people and injures 150

1990

Largest tornado outbreak in state history; 37 tornados touch down, leaving 8 people dead and 221 injured

1996

Snowfall amounts of 12-18 inches (30-45 centimeters) fall across parts of central and southern Indiana; wind gusts of 35 miles per hour (56 kilometers per hour) and heavy snow topple thousands of trees in Hoosier National Forest; power knocked out to 200,000 residents and snowdrifts leave southern Indiana roads impassable for days

Legal Stuff

1915

Indiana adopts the Workmen's Compensation Act and the direct primary election law

1933

The state government reorganizes to give the governor greater powers over state agencies

1963

Indiana adopts a 2% sales tax

Legal Stuff

1965

Department of Natural Resources established to preserve land

1970

Indianapolis merges with Marion County under the Unigov program

1988

State lottery is established

IN ALL FAIRNESS

In 1949, the Indiana legislature passed a law requiring the desegregation of public schools.

UNIFIED LEARNING

In 1959, the General Assembly reorganized the state school system, consolidating small school districts.

IT'S ABOUT TIME

Indiana legislature granted women the right to vote in 1919, one year before the federal government made it law.

WOMEN UNITE

In 1992, the Indiana Commission for Women was formed. Its purpose is to encourage participation of Hoosier women in government, politics, business, education, the judicial system, and all other aspects of life.

Fight!, Fight!, Fight!

Wars the Hoosiers participated in:

- **French and Indian War**
- **Revolutionary War**
- **War of 1812**
- **Civil War**
- **World War I**
- **World War II**
- **Korean War**
- **Vietnam War**
- **Persian Gulf War**

"Ladies and gentlemen, start your engines!"

The revving of car engines and the roar of the crowds can be heard around the Hoosier state on Memorial Day Weekend. It is time for the annual Indianapolis 500 Auto Race! Fans come from near and far to see the biggest and most popular challenge in international auto-racing. With seating for more than 250,000 people in the stands, and thousands more in the infield, the speedway becomes nearly a city of its own.

This spectacular speedway was built in 1909 from 3,200,000 paving bricks. The first race occurred in 1911 and has continued every year since. The track is 2.5 miles (4 kilometers) around and it takes 200 laps to complete the grueling race. The Indy racetrack encircles a large plot of land that includes a golf course and Hall of Fame Museum.

The Indy 500 draws some of the world's top auto racers. Racing greats such as Rick Mears, A.J. Foyt, and Al Unser, Sr. have each won the race four times! Even though these contestants enjoy the thrill of the race, there is another reason they might participate—the prize money is in the millions! In 1994, the NASCAR Brickyard 400 was held at the Indianapolis Motor Speedway for the first time. Hoosier Jeff Gordon has won it twice... so far!

VAROOOOM!

In 1977, Janet Guthrie was the first female racer to compete in the Indy 500.

Indian Tribes

- Miami
- Delaware
- Potawatomi
- Shawnee
- Kickapoo
- Piankashaw
- Wea
- Wyandotte

Many of the Indian tribes lived in houses that consisted of poles stuck in the ground, covered with bark or cattail mats. Patches of deerskin sewn together often served as their clothing.

The longest-lasting and most prominent Native Americans of Indiana were the Miami. They were a deeply religious people who believed in an all-powerful creator, a host of lesser gods, and life after death. To the Miami, good and evil spirits were everywhere—in the rivers, forests, and even in the rocks!

Here, There, Everywhere!

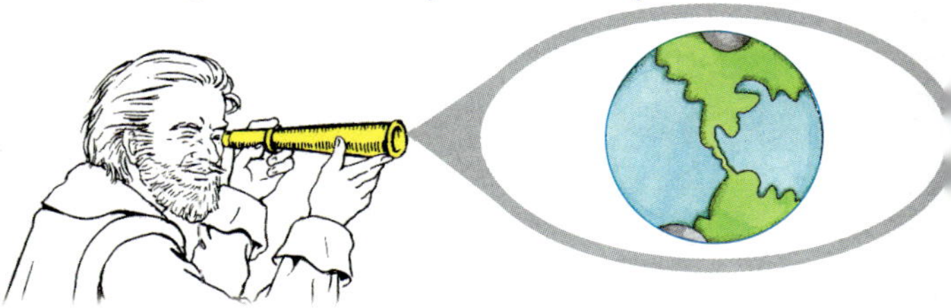

RENÉ-ROBERT CAVELIER, SIEUR DE LA SALLE—French explorer and first known European to pass through Indiana in 1679

ZACHARIAH CICOT—son of a Frenchman and a Potawatomi woman; served as a scout for American army leaders and later founded the town of Independence

FRANCIS GODFROY—part French, part Indian; became a Miami chief and later opened a trading post near the town of Peru

FATHER JACQUES MARQUETTE—member of the Jesuit order of priests; many believed he landed on Indiana's shores even before La Salle

FATHER XAVIER DE GIVINNE—Jesuit priest of the first Christian church in Indiana at Vincennes, 1732

Founding Fathers

These people played especially important roles in early Indiana!

JONATHAN JENNINGS—lawyer, statesman, and first governor of the state of Indiana

ALEXANDER RALSTON—surveyor who laid out plans for the new capital of Indianapolis

GEORGE RAPP—religious leader and founder of Harmonie, a religious settlement of German immigrants in 1815

ROBERT OWEN—wealthy British idealist who bought the Harmonie settlement from George Rapp and renamed it New Harmony; tried to establish the new town as a socialist community in which property and income would be equally shared by all residents, but the community failed

Religious communities, like Harmonie, were common in early Indiana. The founding men and women of these communities were responsible for many new settlements in the state. The different religious settlements included groups of Shakers, Society of Friends (Quakers), African Methodists, Catholics, Amish, and Mennonites. Many of these people and others were also important in starting the first institutions of higher education.

SARAH "MADAME C.J." WALKER—one of the nation's first woman millionaires; developed a conditioning treatment for straightening hair and successfully sold her products door-to-door

RICHARD L. SAXTON—invented a sanitary tissue dispenser for a pay telephone booth

NAOMI BOWMAN TALBERT ANDERSON—feminist and public activist in the mid-to-late 1800s

LILLIAN THOMAS FOX—nationally-recognized reporter and correspondence editor for the *Freeman*, a nationally prominent black newspaper; public speaker and community worker

MINNIE T. SCOTT—pioneer in the Indiana women's club movement who served at state and national levels

SAMUEL SMOTHERS—prominent African-American teacher in the mid-1800s; director of the Union Literary Institute in Randolph County; committed to education and the repeal of the state's Black Laws

BARBARA A. BOYD—first African-American woman on television news in Indiana

VERNA ADAMS—first African-American woman principal of a Fort Wayne Community School; honored by the school system and Lincoln National Bank in 1989 for "an illustrious career which spanned 28 years" by establishing the Verna Adams Scholarship for minority students who want to be teachers

Johnny Appleseed

John Chapman was born in Massachusetts, but traveled throughout the Midwest. He was not poor, but dressed in ragged clothes and was rumored to go barefoot. He found free room and board along the routes he walked. He traveled the midwestern countryside, planting apple seeds that would one day grow into beautiful apple orchards. Does this man sound familiar? You may know him as the beloved folk hero, Johnny Appleseed!

John Chapman died near Fort Wayne in March 1845, due to exposure to the weather. He was buried in Fort Wayne with honors. His gravesite is located in the 43-acre (17.4 hectare) Johnny Appleseed Park. Although this kind and generous sower of seeds died more than 150 years ago, Americans still remember him fondly, especially in the Hoosier state.

Ask an adult to help you with the following recipe.

APPLE CRISP

6 medium size cooking apples
3/4 cup brown sugar
3/4 cup rolled oats
1/4 cup butter
1/8 teaspoon salt

Directions:

Preheat oven to 350°F (177 °C). Grease pan lightly. Cut and peel apples and slice thin. Mix rolled oats, sugar, and butter with your fingers until crumbly. Put mixture on apples in pan. Bake for 35 minutes. Enjoy!

Sports Stuff

Famous Hoosier Sports Figures:

BOBBY KNIGHT—Indiana University's controversial and fiery basketball coach from 1971-2000; won 11 Big 10 Conference titles; coached gold-medal teams in the 1979 Pan American Games and the 1984 Olympic Games

KNUTE ROCKNE—University of Notre Dame football player and later head coach who led the Fighting Irish in an amazing number of victories between 1918 and 1930; considered a football innovator in every way

FOUR HORSEMEN—Notre Dame's all-American backfield, nicknamed by sportswriter Grantland Rice in 1924

JAYME DICKMAN—gold medalist in air rifle and three-position rifle at 1999 Pan American Games; bronze medalist in both events at 1999 World Championships

MELISSA RYAN—silver medalist (1996) and bronze medalist (2000) in Olympic Pairs Rowing Event

JOHN WOODEN—all-American guard for Purdue's basketball team; became UCLA's head coach in the 1960s

LARRY BIRD—a French Lick basketball superstar; played 13 years for the Boston Celtics; returned to Indiana to coach the Indiana Pacers in 1997; inducted into the Naismith Memorial Basketball Hall of Fame in 1998

MARK SPITZ—one of the greatest Olympic swimmers of all time; captured a record seven gold medals at the 1972 Olympic games

JEFF GORDON—NASCAR great; won several titles, including the Winston Cup and the Brickyard 400 at the Indianapolis Motor Speedway

Entertainers

Herb Shriner based many of his jokes on his love for the Hoosier state. One famous Shriner quote was, "I was born in Ohio, but moved to Indiana as soon as I heard about it."

★ Herb Shriner—comedian, radio and television host

★ Hoagy Carmichael—songwriter, pianist

★ John Cougar Mellencamp—singer, songwriter

★ Michael Jackson—singer

★ Phil Harris—actor, band leader, radio host during the 1940s

★ James Dean—popular movie star of the 1950s

★ Leon Ames, Buck Jones, Forrest Tucker, Steve McQueen—actors

★ David Letterman—TV host, comedian

★ James McCracken—tenor

★ Shelley Long, Anne Baxter, Carole Lombard, Marjorie Main—actresses

★ Cole Porter—songwriter

★ Ned Rorem—composer

★ Red Skelton—comedian

★ Twyla Tharp—dancer, choreographer

★ Paul Dresser—songwriter

★ Jane Pauley—TV journalist; former host of "The Today Show" and "Dateline"

★ Janet Jackson—singer, actress

RIDDLE: I am the famous songwriter who wrote the musicals *Kiss Me, Kate* and *Can-Can*. Who am I?

ANSWER: Cole Porter

Authors

Indiana has produced more great writers than any other state of equal size.

- **James Whitcomb Riley**—Poet Laureate of Indiana who wrote about his rural Hoosier childhood in poems such as "Little Orphant Annie"
- **George Ade**—humorist and poet
- **Joaquin Miller**—poet
- **Rex Stout**—mystery writer
- **Ernest Taylor Pyle**—journalist during WWII; became America's most popular war correspondent; won Pulitzer Prize in 1944 for foreign correspondence
- **Kurt Vonnegut, Jr.**—author who wrote *Cat's Cradle* and *Slaughterhouse Five*
- **Booth Tarkington**—Pulitzer Prize winner for *Magnificent Ambersons*
- **Jessamyn West**—author; famous for her moving novel *The Friendly Persuasion*
- **John Finley**—writer and poet
- **Lew Wallace**—writer of the best-selling novel *Ben-Hur*
- **Ross Lockridge**—author whose historical novel *Raintree County* became a movie
- **Irving Leibowitz**—critic and writer who wrote a bittersweet account of Hoosier life in the novel *My Indiana*
- **Jim Davis**—cartoonist; creator of the *Garfield* comic strip
- **John Soule**—Hoosier journalist; first to print the phrase "Go West, young man" in 1851
- **Mary Jane Ward**—author of *The Snake Pit,* which exposed the unfair and inhumane practices of mental institutions

Hoosier Artists

Jacob Cox—Civil-War artist and art teacher

George Winter—Englishman who came to Indiana in 1837 and painted landscapes of the Wabash River country

Charles Alexander Lesueur—made sketches of settlers and settlements

Otto Stark, John Bundy, William Forsyth—these artists' style came to be known as the Indiana school of painting, which celebrated nature in romantic landscapes; also termed the "Hoosier Group"

Hale Woodruff, John Hardrick, William Scott—three black artists of the early 1900s, influenced by the Hoosier Group

Robert Indiana (Clark)—modern artist and sculptor who changed his last name to show his Hoosier pride

Mary Beth Edelson, Robert Berkshire—contemporary painters

Theodore C. Steele—Brown County artist

"I insist that the Hoosier is different mentally and spiritually from the average American… He has the temperament of the artist."

—Theodore Dreiser

Very Important People

FRANK BORMAN—astronaut, commanded first space flight to orbit the moon; airline executive and chairman of the board of Eastern Airlines

AMBROSE EVERETT BURNSIDE—Army officer, inventor, politician; commanded troops during the Civil War; his beard style became origin of the term "sideburns"; governor of Rhode Island; U.S. senator

EUGENE VICTOR DEBS—labor leader who established the Industrial Workers of the World labor union; ran five times for U.S. president as a Socialist

REVEREND JACQUELINE EHRINGER MEANS—first woman in the U.S. officially ordained a priest in the Episcopal Church, in 1977

VIRGIL IVAN "GUS" GRISSOM—astronaut

PAUL ANTHONY SAMUELSON—economist who won the Nobel Prize in 1970

HAROLD CLAYTON UREY—chemist who won the 1934 Nobel Prize in chemistry

WENDELL LEWIS WILLKIE—lawyer, politician, financier; known as the "Barefoot boy on Wall Street"; ran against Roosevelt in 1940 on the Republican ticket

BILL BLASS—fashion designer

COLONEL ELI LILLY—founder of Eli Lilly and Company in 1876, a research-based pharmaceutical (medicine) company

BALL BROTHERS—five brothers who moved their Indiana glass products company to Muncie in 1887

JUDY H. SINGLETON—businesswoman, political activist, writer; named one of Indianapolis' "Most Influential Women" in 1997; author of *Indiana's Trailblazing Women*

Inventors

Wilbur Wright—inventor, along with his brother, of the first self-propelled airplane

Marcella Gruelle—inventor of the Raggedy Ann doll in 1914

Clement and John Studebaker—manufactured wagons and carriages; later made Studebaker automobiles

Gilbert Van Camp—created a family recipe for pork and beans in tomato sauce; opened up a canning company to sell Van Camp's Pork and Beans

James Oliver—inventor of the first chilled-steel plow

Ambrose Everett Burnside—created the breech-loading rifle

Sylvanus F. Bowser—designed the world's first practical gasoline pump

Richard Gatling—inventor of the rapid-fire machine gun in 1862

Elwood Haynes—created first successful gasoline-powered, clutch-driven automobile

GOOD GUYS

ARTHUR BANTA was a zoologist who gained recognition for his studies of environmental effects on cave animals.

ALBERT BEVERIDGE was a politician, historian, and U.S. senator from Indiana. He drafted a meat-inspection bill, fought for child-labor laws, and voted against high tariff rates. In 1920, he won a Pulitzer Prize in biography for *The Life of John Marshall*.

GEORGE FREDERICK DICK was a physician who, along with his wife Gladys, isolated the bacterium that causes scarlet fever. Scarlet fever was a leading cause of death in children before the 1900s.

BAD GUYS

JIMMY HOFFA was a famous labor leader and president of the Teamsters Union. He was imprisoned in 1967 for misusing union pension funds and was released in 1971. He disappeared in 1975, and it is believed that he was murdered.

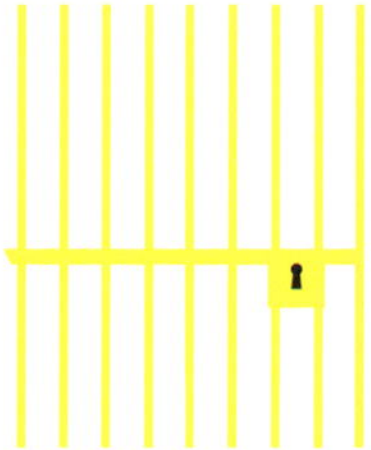

In 1934, the notorious Chicago gangster, **JOHN DILLINGER**, escaped the Lake County Jail in Crown Point by using a "pistol" he had carved from a block of wood!

Speaking of bad guys and jails, Crawfordsville is the home of the only known working rotary jail in the U.S. The jail has a rotating cellblock and was built in 1882. It served as the Montgomery County Jail until 1972. It is now a museum!

Political Leaders

Abraham Lincoln

ABRAHAM LINCOLN—sixteenth president of the United States; spent boyhood in Spencer County before moving to Illinois to become a lawyer and statesman

BIRCH BAYH, JR.—U.S. senator; won nationwide attention for his opposition to the Vietnam War

OTIS RAY "DOC" BOWEN—first Indiana governor to serve two consecutive terms; U.S. secretary of Health and Human Services

SCHUYLER COLFAX—U.S. representative from Indiana; speaker of the house; vice-president of the U.S.

SUE ANNE GILROY—first woman Indiana secretary of state

CHARLES WARREN FAIRBANKS—U.S. senator; U.S. vice-president

BENJAMIN HARRISON—twenty-third president of the United States

WILLIAM HENRY HARRISON—ninth president of the United States; governor of Territory of Indiana; defeated Indians at the Battle of Tippecanoe

RICHARD HATCHER—mayor of Gary; one of the first black mayors of a big city

JOHN MILTON HAY—U.S. secretary of state

THOMAS ANDREWS HENDRICKS—U.S. representative from Indiana; U.S. senator; governor; U.S. vice-president

JONATHAN JENNINGS—first governor of the state of Indiana

RICHARD LUGAR—mayor of Indianapolis; U.S. senator

THOMAS RILEY MARSHALL—governor; U.S. vice-president

OLIVER HAZARD PERRY THROCK MORTON—governor; U.S. senator

ROBERT DALE OWEN—U.S. representative from Indiana; led the fight for emancipation of black slaves

JAMES DANFORTH QUAYLE—U.S. representative from Indiana; U.S. vice-president

WILLIS VAN DEVANTER—associate justice of the U.S. Supreme Court

Churches and Schools

Keeping the Faith

Basilica of St. Francis Xavier, Vincennes

First Christian Church, Columbus—designed by famous architect Eliel Saarinen and completed in 1942

Christ Church Cathedral, Indianapolis—built in 1857 and the oldest church building in continuous use in the city; features Tiffany Studio windows

Saint John Catholic Church and Rectory, Indianapolis—oldest Catholic church and parish in the city; established in 1867

SCHOOLS

Many private colleges in Indiana were started by religious groups. Below are a few public and private universities and colleges in Indiana.

- **Indiana University**, Bloomington—largest institution of higher education in the state; various campuses throughout the state; chartered as Indiana Seminary in 1820
- **Hanover College**, Madison—founded by Presbyterians in 1827
- **Purdue University**, West Lafayette—premier engineering school; chartered as a land-grant college in 1865; various campuses throughout the state
- **University of Notre Dame**, South Bend—one of the top Roman Catholic schools in the world, founded in 1842
- **Rose-Hulman Institute of Technology**, Terre Haute
- **Indiana State University**, Terre Haute—founded in 1865
- **Earlham College**, Richmond—Quaker college founded in 1847

Indiana's state constitution of 1816 was the first in the U.S. to provide a system of free public schools from the elementary to the university level. However, the state could not provide the tax money to build these schools until the 1850s. In the meantime, some parents chipped in to build and pay for their own community schools!

Full of Hoosier History!

★ **LINCOLN BOYHOOD NATIONAL MEMORIAL,** Lincoln City

★ **WHITEWATER CANAL STATE HISTORIC SITE,** Metamora—experience a horse-drawn canal boat ride

★ **GEORGE ROGERS CLARK NATIONAL HISTORIC PARK,** Vincennes—commemorates the Revolutionary War hero's capture of Fort Sackville in 1779, the largest land conquest of the American Revolution

Abraham Lincoln

★ **CORYDON CAPITOL STATE HISTORIC SITE,** Corydon—served as Indiana's first capital; nearby governor's residence and old town square also preserved as state historic sites

★ **T.C. STEELE HISTORIC SITE,** Belmont—artist's eleven-room home, studio, cabin, and wildflower gardens

★ **ERNIE PYLE STATE HISTORIC SITE,** Dana—farmhome of well-known World War II correspondent Ernie Pyle

★ **DENTZEL CAROUSEL NATIONAL HISTORIC LANDMARK,** Indianapolis—housed in the Children's Museum of Indianapolis

★ **ANGEL MOUNDS STATE HISTORIC SITE,** near Evansville

★ **LIMBERLOST STATE HISTORIC SITE,** Geneva

★ **GENE STRATTON PORTER STATE HISTORIC SITE,** near Rome City

★ **INDIANA TERRITORY STATE HISTORIC SITE,** Vincennes

Historic Hoosier Town

The town of Madison is known for its historic homes. Due to its incredible architecture, an astounding 133 square blocks of the town are listed on the National Register of Historic Places!

Early Residency

★ **Levi Coffin House**, Fountain City—Quaker home of Levi and Katie Coffin; famous stop on the Underground Railroad

★ **Grouseland**, Vincennes—home of William Henry Harrison

★ **Abraham Lincoln's Boyhood Home**, Lincoln City

★ **Owen House**, New Harmony—built in 1830

★ **President Benjamin Harrison Home**, Indianapolis—mansion built in 1875

★ **Culbertson Mansion**, New Albany—pale yellow brick structure built in 1867; part of Mansion Row Historic District

★ **Grisamore House**, Jeffersonville—built in 1837 as a double residence for both David and Wilson Grisamore

★ **Lanier House**, Madison—built from 1840 to 1844; overlooks the Ohio River

Home, Sweet Home!

★ **Shrewsbury House**, Madison—built between 1846 and 1849; contains a three-story freestanding spiral staircase

★ **J.K. Lilly Mansion**, Indianapolis—located on the 154-acre (62-hectare) estate of the grandson of Eli Lilly; now part of the Indianapolis Museum of Art

★ **James Whitcomb Riley House**, Indianapolis—the 1872 Italianate home of the famous Hoosier poet

Forts & Battles

A few of Indiana's famous forts

- **Fort Ouiatenon,** south of Lafayette
- **Fort Miami**, city of Fort Wayne
- **Fort Vincennes**, city of Vincennes

These three French forts were the first permanent European settlements in Indiana.

A few of Indiana's famous battles

During **Pontiac's Rebellion**, Ottawa chief Pontiac overtook Fort Ouiatenon and Fort Miami in Indiana. However, he was unable to ultimately win this rebellion against the British because his warriors could not conquer the important Great Lakes fort at Detroit.

The **Battle of Fort Sackville** occurred near Vincennes in 1779. The American troops, led by famous George Rogers Clark, defeated British troops led by Henry "Hair Buyer" Hamilton, to win back Fort Sackville.

The **Battle of Tippecanoe** occurred in 1811 near present-day Lafayette. Tecumseh's Indian confederation, led by his brother the Shawnee Prophet, was defeated by General William Henry Harrison's troops.

Libraries

Hoosiers love to read! Indiana libraries have the highest circulation rate among the states.

- **Indianapolis Public Library**—largest in the state
- **Indiana State Library**—Indianapolis
- **Indianapolis-Marion County Library**—known for its architecture, it is ranked as one of the best Classical buildings in the country
- **Willard Library, Evansville**—oldest public library building; the children's and reference section are said to be haunted by the Grey Lady!
- **Old Cathedral Library**, Vincennes—holds many rare books printed before 1800
- **Lilly Library, Bloomington**—holds thousands of rare books, including a Gutenberg Bible
- **Indiana University-Purdue University at Indianapolis Library**

The libraries at Notre Dame, Purdue, DePauw, and Indiana University all have several special collections.

One of the first circulating Indiana libraries was the Mount Pleasant Library, part of the African Methodist Episcopal (AME) church. This library served both black and white citizens from 1842 to 1867.

Zoos & Attractions

- **Indianapolis Zoo**—a 64-acre zoo (26-hectare) that is arranged in "biomes," or collections of habitats
- **Menno-Hof Mennonite-Amish Visitors Center**, Shipshewana—tells about the history, beliefs, and lifestyle of the Mennonite and Amish people
- **Inland Aquatics**, Terre Haute—contains largest coral reef display in the U.S.
- **Imagination Station**, Lafayette—hands-on science experiments for kids
- **West Baden Springs Hotel**, West Baden—early 1900s resort visited by the rich and famous; contains a huge atrium dome, larger than that of the U.S. Capitol; closed down during the Depression; currently being restored for resale
- **Amish Acres**, Nappanee—restored Amish farm where visitors take tours of the house and barn, watch craft demonstrations, and take buggy rides
- **Conner Prairie**, Noblesville—an 1836 restored pioneer village where costumed "settlers" go about their jobs and games
- **Sugar Creek**, Crawfordsville—for canoe enthusiasts; venture down the calms and rapids of this beautiful waterway
- **Mesker Park Zoo**, Evansville—houses more than 700 animals; features a botanical garden and butterfly exhibit in the summer
- **Lincoln Pioneer Village**, Rockport—home of rustic log buildings and two museums that commemorate Abraham Lincoln's childhood days spent in Indiana
- **New Harmony Settlement**—preserves the settlements of the Harmonists and Owenites

Museums

- **Indiana Basketball Hall of Fame Museum**, New Castle
- **Lincoln Museum**, Fort Wayne—contains world's largest private collection of Abraham Lincoln memorabilia
- **Auburn-Cord-Duesenberg Museum**, Auburn—displays many classic cars
- **Studebaker National Museum**, South Bend—displays Studebaker cars, as well as other vehicles of the century
- **Indiana Military Museum**, Vincennes—contains collections that cover U.S. military history from the Civil War to the Gulf War

- **Indianapolis Children's Museum**, Indianapolis—world's largest museum for kids
- **Indiana Railway Museum**, French Lick—gives train rides through part of the Hoosier National Forest
- **Indiana State Museum**, Indianapolis
- **Wayne County Historical Museum**, Richmond—recognized as one of the best county museums in the state; collections range from vintage cars to a 3,000-year-old mummy
- **Children's Museum**, Muncie—hands-on museum with Garfield the Cat attractions
- **Indianapolis Motor Speedway Hall of Fame Museum**, contains many Indy 500 winning cars as well as a collection of antique and classic passenger cars
- **International Circus Hall of Fame Museum**, Peru

State Parks

- **Falls of the Ohio State Park**, near Madison—home of 400-million-year-old fossil beds
- **Brown County State Park**, east of Bloomington—state's largest park; very popular with tourists and landscape painters
- **McCormick's Creek State Park**, northwest of Bloomington—first state park established in Indiana
- **Turkey Run State Park**, west central Indiana—noted for its rugged sandstone canyons and winding streams
- **Spring Mill State Park**, Mitchell—home of some of the state's largest tulip trees and white oaks; site of restored frontier village
- **Clifty Falls State Park**, southeastern Indiana—areas of the park present beautiful views of the Ohio River and Kentucky shoreline
- **Mounds State Park**, east of Anderson—contains the state's largest Native American earthworks
- **Pokagon State Park**, Angola—popular center for winter sports

Memorials

Soldiers and Sailors Monument
Indianapolis

Tippecanoe Battlefield Monument
Lafayette

Battle of Corydon Memorial Park
Corydon

Johnny Appleseed Memorial Park
Fort Wayne

The Show Must Go On!

Brown County Artist Colony, formed in the early 1900s in the Hoosier town of Nashville

Indiana Repertory Theater, Indianapolis—plays in a refurbished downtown movie palace

Indianapolis Symphony Orchestra—founded in 1930; considered one of the finest in the Midwest; headquartered in Circle Theatre, a beautifully restored concert hall

Arthur Jordan College of Music—part of Butler University; training site for many young classical musicians

Indianapolis Museum of Art—Indiana's main museum of art

Eiteljorg Museum of American Indian and Western Art, Indianapolis—contains art from the early 1800s to the present

Open-air Playhouse, Nashville—hosts performances by Indiana University students

Sand Dunes

Indiana Dunes National Lakeshore

Indiana may not be able to claim the majestic Rockies or the Grand Canyon, but the state can claim the largest sand dunes this side of the Sahara Desert! The sand dunes were created from glacial deposits. *The Indiana Dunes National Lakeshore* is situated on Lake Michigan, between Michigan City and Gary. It is a 13,000-acre (5,261-hectare) natural wonder in the middle of one of the most heavily industrialized regions in the country. It boasts lovely beaches, hiking, biking, and horseback-riding trails. However, the incredible sand dunes are what draw many visitors. Mt. Baldy is a 135-foot (41-meter) tall sand dune. Visitors like to climb to the top to get a sweeping view of Lake Michigan.

Completely surrounded by the national lakeshore is the *Indiana Dunes State Park*. It covers 2,182 acres (883 hectares) and boasts the highest sand dune along the lakeshore—192-foot (58-meter) tall Mt. Tom. If you listen carefully, sometimes you can hear a low, humming sound made by the drifting sands. These unique and soothing sounds are known locally as the music of the "singing sands."

HISTORIC and SCENIC ROADS

The **National Road** was Indiana's first interstate highway. The National Road was also known as the Cumberland Road. This 600-mile (965-kilometer) road ran from Vandalia, Illinois to Cumberland, Maryland and took thirty years to build! **U.S. Route 40** now follows the route of the National Road.

U.S. 20 and **Routes 16, 250N,** and **200N** ramble along through Amish Country in Indiana. This drive features well-groomed farms and quaint villages, as well as a close look at the religious community of the Amish.

The **Ohio River Scenic Route** runs from Aurora to Madison on **Indiana 56** and **156**. It follows the great Ohio River for 57 miles (92 kilometers). Travelers can also view the bountiful tobacco fields that dot the landscape.

The **Lincoln Hills Scenic Drive** meanders along **Indiana 62** from Corydon to Dale. Part of the drive passes through the rolling hills of Hoosier National Forest.

Caves & Caverns

In southern Indiana it is common to see caves and caverns (especially large caves). The natural acids in rain and snow worked to dissolve the abundant limestone underground to form hollowed-out caves and underground streams.

BIG BLUE

Bluespring Cavern, near Bedford, is one of the ten largest caves in the world. This cavern is home to the longest "lost river" in the country. Most of the cavern's miles are underground streams. Visitors ride in flat-bottomed boats to explore.

CATHEDRAL CAVE

Wyandotte Cave, near Leavenworth, is one of the largest caves in North America. It has more than 35 miles (56 kilometers) of underground passageways. Inside Wyandotte Cave is a huge chamber called Rothrock Cathedral. It got its name from a large limestone "mountain" that rises 135 feet (41 meters) high!

DANCE HALL DAYS

North of Wyandotte Cave lies **Marengo Cave.** This cave houses a magnificent underground room called the Crystal Palace. Underground weddings and dances in the cave have been common over the years. Each July a square dance is held in the cave's Music Hall Chamber!

GRAVE CAVE

The **Squire Boone Caverns** near Corydon, were discovered by Daniel Boone and his brother Squire. Squire settled in the area, and when he died, residents honored his dying wish, to be buried in the cave. The cave has been called the most dazzling cave around. It contains a wonderful mix of colorful stalactites and stalagmites as well as underground streams and waterfalls.

Animals of Indiana

Red Fox
White-tailed Deer
Muskrat
Raccoon
Mink
Squirrel
Opossum
Woodchuck
Gopher
Rabbit
Skunk
Weasel
Chipmunk

Take A Walk On the Wild Side

The buffalo that once lived in Indiana disappeared because of large-scale settlement of the state during the 1800s. Black bear, elk, lynx, mountain lions, wolverines, and porcupines were all once part of Indiana's wildlife. They have gradually decreased in number due to overhunting and habitat destruction. They can no longer be found in the wild in Indiana.

Some of the animals that still live in the Hoosier state, but are in danger of becoming extinct are the badger, bobcat, river otter, gray and red wolves, and several types of bat.

"Extinct" means that something has died out, or ceased to exist. Many animal species that are in danger of becoming extinct are protected by state and federal laws.

You May Spy These Birds in Indiana:

Blue Jay
Sparrow
Wren
Swallow
Warbler
Oriole
Wood Thrush
Cardinal
Dove
Crow
Meadowlark
Chickadee
Hawk
Owl
Quail
Turkey
Pheasant
Ruffed Grouse
Mallard
Goose
Wood Duck

Wood duck

Indiana's endangered bird species include bald eagles, peregrine falcons, piping plovers, trumpeter swans, and yellow-headed blackbirds.

Don't let these Indiana bugs bug you!

Mayfly

Dragonfly

Katydid

Cricket

Stick Insect

Cicada

Beetle

Firefly

Moth

Mosquito

Honeybee

Yellow Jacket

Bumblebee

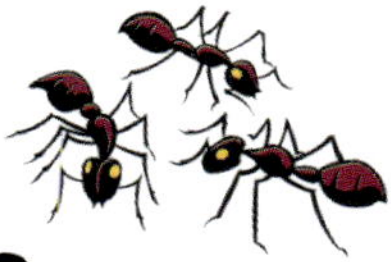
Ants

Butterfly

Praying Mantis

Ladybug

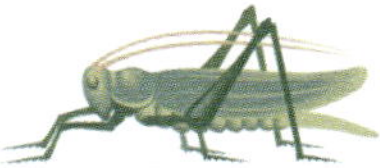
Grasshopper

Some ants capture the young of other ants and make them work as slaves!

Swimming in Indiana Waters:

Carp
Catfish
Bowfin
Smallmouth Bass
Bluegill
Largemouth
Black Bass
Sunfish
Gar
Pike
Pickerel
Salmon
Trout

Pond Critters

In Indiana's ponds, you may find:

Hydra
Leech
Freshwater Mussel
Snail
Water Flea
Freshwater Crayfish
Fishing Spider
Water Bug
Water Strider
Whirligig Beetle
Freshwater Eel
Turtle
Water Snake
Mud Puppy
Newt
Toad
Frog

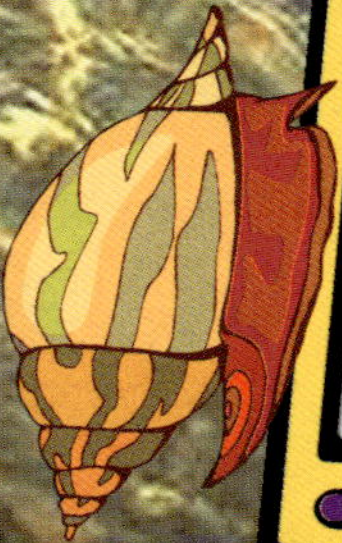

A water snake may dangle from a low-hanging tree branch, waiting for the right moment to pounce on his prey!

Rocks & Minerals

Minerals are the building blocks of all rocks. A mineral can be as large as a person, but most are tiny and you will need a magnifying glass to see them clearly. Below are a few types of minerals that can be found in Indiana.

Quartz

Iron Pyrite
Quartz
Calcite
Feldspar
Kaolinite

Rocks are solid masses of minerals or rock fragments that occur in nature. Below are a few types of rock that can be found in Indiana.

Sandstone

Limestone

Sandstone
Mudstone
Shale
Limestone
Peat
Quartzite
Meteorites

TREEMENDOUS!

These trees grace the Hoosier state:

Sycamore
Maple
Poplar
Dogwood
Beech
Hickory
Ash
Elm
Walnut
Cedar
Locust
Birch
Tulip Tree
Sweet Gum
Hemlock
Cottonwood
Oak

The Council Oak Tree, located in South Bend's Highland Cemetery, is a historical tree. In 1681, on a second trip on the St. Joseph River, La Salle met with the chiefs of the Miami and their neighbors, the Illinois. He tried to persuade the two groups to unite and stand against the powerful Iroquois of the East, who were allies of the British. However, the two tribes did not agree to join forces. The Council Oak Tree is believed to have been a "witness" to that historic meeting between La Salle and the Indians. If true, this ancient oak tree is more than 300 years old!

Flowers

Peony	Sunflower	Buttercup
Wild Lupine	Wild Rose	Chicory
Wood Anemone	Trillium	Pitcher Plant
Daisy	Geranium	Milkweed
Goldenrod	Lady's Slipper	Violet
Aster	Black-eyed Susan	
Queen Anne's Lace	Indian Paintbrush	

Cream of the Crops

Agricultural products from Indiana.

Tomatoes

Wheat

Ducks

Sheep

Beef Cattle

Popcorn

Blueberries

Corn

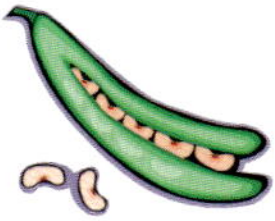

Snap Beans

Peppermint and Spearmint

Hogs

Cucumbers

Soybeans

Apples

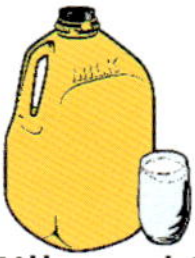

Milk and Ice Cream

Tobacco

Hoosier Potpourri

THE UNIVERSITY OF NOTRE DAME'S LIBRARY has a famous landmark mosaic that is a favorite with football fans. This gigantic mosaic features Jesus with upraised arms and has been called the "Touchdown Jesus."

SANTA CLAUS, Indiana receives over half a million letters and requests at Christmas time.

Peru, Indiana was once known as the "CIRCUS CAPITAL OF AMERICA."

TV talk-show host OPRAH WINFREY has had a country retreat in Indiana for over 10 years. She calls it her "favorite place in all the world."

The SATURDAY EVENING POST is published in Indianapolis.

Indiana is the national leader in production of MUSICAL INSTRUMENTS.

Jim Davis, the CREATOR OF GARFIELD THE CARTOON CAT, now lives in a house without cats because his wife is allergic to them!

Wabash was the FIRST ELECTRICALLY LIGHTED CITY.

There are only three ROLLS-ROYCE car dealerships in the U.S.—one in Beverly Hills, California; one in New York City; and one in Zionsville, Indiana!

Sandy Allen of Shelbyville is the TALLEST LIVING WOMAN in the world. She stands 7 feet, 7 and 1/4 inches (2.31 meters). Sandy sews most of her own clothes and wears size 22 hand-me-down sneakers provided by the players in the NBA!

Festivals

Johnny Appleseed Festival, Fort Wayne

James Whitcomb Riley Festival, Greenfield

The Indy Festival, Indianapolis

Popcorn Festival, Valparaiso

Bluegrass Festival, Indianapolis

Indiana State Fair, Brevard

Harvest Homecoming, New Albany

Rose Festival, Richmond

Mushroom Festival, Mansfield

Glass Festival, Greentown

Freedom Festival, Evansville

Turkey Trot Festival, Daviess County

Wizard of Oz Festival, Chesterton

Holidays

Calendar

Martin Luther King, Jr. Day, *3rd Monday in January*

Presidents' Day, *3rd Monday in February*

George Rogers Clark Day, *February 25*

Memorial Day, *last Monday in May*

Independence Day, *July 4*

Labor Day, *1st Monday in September*

Columbus Day, *2nd Monday in October*

Veterans Day, *November 11*

Thanksgiving, *the 4th Thursday in November*

Indiana Day, *December 11*

Christmas, *December 25*

Hoosier Foods

Indiana's Fabulous Foods!

- Perch
- Meatloaf
- Breaded Pork Tenderloin Sandwich
- Rhubarb Pie
- Beef and Noodles
- Apple Cider
- Apple Crisp
- Poke Sallet
- Dandelion Greens
- Pan-fried Fish
- Maple Sugar Candy
- Persimmon Pudding
- Fried Morel Mushrooms

Indiana Works!

Northern Indiana is known for its industry. The area known as the *Calumet Region* includes Whiting, Burns Harbor, East Chicago, Gary, and Hammond. This region borders Lake Michigan and is one of the world's greatest industrial centers. It includes steel mills, oil refineries, cement plants, and numerous factories.

Manufacturing is the state's most important industry and biggest employer. Indiana is the top steel-producing state and one of the world's leading steel centers. Aluminum is another important metal manufactured in the state. Factories throughout the state make parts for motor vehicles and airplanes, industrial machinery, rubber and plastic products, electronic and electrical equipment. Chemical production, from paint to prescription drugs, is also important in the Hoosier state.

Some popular manufacturing companies in Indiana include Eli Lilly, U.S. Steel, General Motors, and Jayco Recreational Vehicles.

State Books & Websites

America the Beautiful: Indiana
From Sea to Shining Sea: Indiana
Hello USA: Indiana
Let's Discover the States: Indiana
Off the Beaten Path: Indiana
Indiana Jeopardy! by Carole Marsh
My First Book About Indiana by Carole Marsh
The Indiana Experience Series by Carole Marsh

Indiana Glossary

Glossary Words

confederacy: a union of people, groups, or states for a certain purpose
dune: rounded hill or ridge of sand that has been heaped up by the wind
heartland: central region that is important economically or politically
immigrant: person who comes to a new country to live
legend: story handed down through the years; may be partly true
manufacture: the making of goods and articles, especially in large amounts by machinery
mound: a heap or bank of earth or sand; little hill
orchard: a piece of land where fruit or nut trees are grown
revolution: the overthrow of a government
secede: to voluntarily give up being part of an organized group
spelunker: a person who explores caves
union: group of nations, people, etc...joined together in a larger unit for some common purpose

Indiana Spelling Bee

Here are some special Indiana-related words to learn! To take the Spelling Bee, have someone call out the words and you spell them aloud or write them on a piece of paper.

Spelling Words		
	Amish	Nappanee
	Calumet	Pokagon
	Duesenberg	Potawatomi
	Eiteljorg	Salamonie
	Hoosier	Shawnee
	Leavenworth	Shipshewana
	Maumee	Tecumseh
	Mennonite	Tippecanoe
	Mississinewa	Wawasee

ABOUT THE AUTHOR...

CAROLE MARSH has been writing about Indiana for more than 20 years. She is the author of the popular Indiana State Stuff series for young readers and creator, along with her son, Michael Marsh, of "Indiana Facts and Factivities," a CD-ROM widely used in Indiana schools. The author of more than 100 Indiana books and other supplementary educational materials on the state, Marsh is currently working on a new collection of Indiana materials for young people. Marsh correlates her Indiana materials to the Indiana Academic Standards. Many of her books and other materials have been inspired by or requested by Indiana teachers and librarians.

EDITORIAL ASSISTANT AND FORMER HOOSIER: JILL SANDERS

GRAPHIC DESIGNER: CECIL ANDERSON